INDIAN METAL SCULPTURE

INDIAN
METAL SCULPTURE

by

CHINTAMONI KAR

1952

ALEC TIRANTI LTD.

72 CHARLOTTE STREET,
LONDON, W.1

PREFACE

This little book has no pretension of being treated as a complete history of Indian metal sculpture. So far, very little has been written on the subject. There have been practically no scholarly investigations, and the student must undertake his own researches. A comprehensive study of Indian metal art should deal not only with work from India proper, but also with the metal statuaries of China, Burma, Siam, Cambodia, Ceylon, Java, Sumatra and Bali, all of which were deeply influenced by India. From very ancient time these lands came in direct contact with Indian religion, art, and folk-lore. Some of the old Indian traditions and religious institutions which no longer exist in India today are still very much alive in these countries. For centuries, in the past, a great number of Indian metal statues were imported into these distant lands, and there they served as models and ideals to inspire the local craftsmen in making the images of gods and goddesses. To study and write extensively on the history of Indianesque metal sculpture in these lands would be the task of a lifetime.

Most of the Indian metal figures have been commonly described as bronzes by many experts on the subject. But the majority of them are not made of the alloy which is commonly known as bronze. Few of the Indian metal figures have yet been chemically analysed. By ordinary visual examination it is extremely difficult to distinguish between the gilt copper and gilt bronze or brass, or between corroded copper and bronze or brass. Many Indian metal images have been given a very early date simply because of their antique appearance, but further scientific and detailed examination may quite possibly prove that they belong to late periods.

The examples reproduced in this book should not be taken as exhausting the different types of Indian metal sculpture.

No photographs are available of many metal figures, some of them of great historical importance, which have left India and are in possession of collectors all over the world. Many interesting specimens are still stored in the cellars of important museum and art collections in Western countries, and critics and students cannot easily view them. Other magnificent metal images are still worshipped in the sanctum of the Indian temples and it is not an easy matter to obtain photographs of these.

The political history which is the background of the story of metal art has been very much condensed to fit into a book of this size, which is intended purely as a concise guide to the subject. Readers wishing further information on the subject will perhaps find the short bibliography useful.

The author owes thanks to the authorities of the Royal Academy of Arts, British Museum, Indian Section of the Victoria and Albert Museum in London, and National Museum, Copenhagen, Museum of Fine Arts, Boston, Archaeological Survey of India and the Trustees of the Indian Museum, Calcutta, for their generous permission to reproduce the photographs of pieces in their collections. He is also grateful to Mr. John Irwin and the personnel of the Indian Section Victoria and Albert Museum, Mr. D. E. Barret of the Oriental Antiquities Department, British Museum, Mr. C. B. Rao of the Government of India Ministry of Information and Broadcasting, and Mr. Christmas Humphreys for helping him to obtain photographs of pieces specially photographed for this book. He also acknowledges with thanks the kind help received from the personnel of the India Office Library, Commonwealth Relations Office, London, while using the library. The author owes special thanks to Mr. Guy Wint for reading the manuscript.

LONDON, 1952.   C. K.

CONTENTS

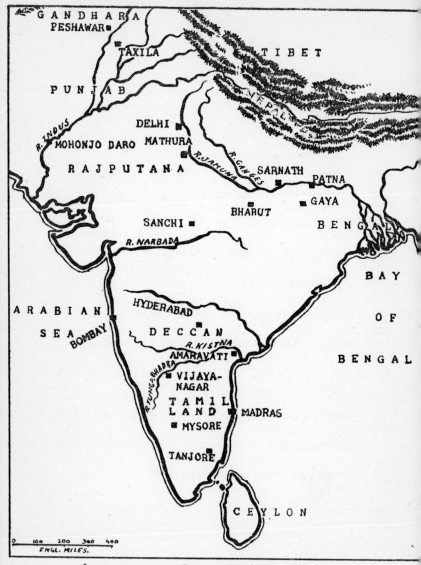

INDIA, SHOWING THE SITES OF THE ANCIENT MONUMENTS

I

The Antiquity of Indian Metal Craft.

METAL and alloys were used for works of art in India from very ancient time. A small bronze statuette of a dancing girl found in the buried city of Mohonjo Daro in Sindh shows that the process of lost-wax (*cire perdue*) was known to India some five thousand years ago and that it was already carried out with great skill and artistry. There must have been a long anterior period of development of metal crafts in the country before such a level of artistic performance could be reached. But specimens of the art have not survived. Besides this single example from Mohonjo Daro there are no ancient metal figures of artistic value which can be dated before the beginning of the Christian era.

Many different metals and alloys were used in ancient India. Dr. Coomaraswamy, the great Ceylonese writer on Indian art, said: "Not only was iron worked at an early date (being mentioned with gold, silver, lead and tin in Yajur Veda), but there existed (and perhaps originated) in India a very early knowledge of the art of preparing steel; the steel of India was known to the Greeks and Persians, and very probably to the Egyptians, as was also the material of the famous blades of Damascus."

Pure copper was widely used in India for works of art from the earliest times. Bronze, which is commonly understood as an alloy consisting of copper with about one part in ten of tin, was more rarely used. The reasons for this are not clear. There are records that gold and silver also were used in ancient India to produce large sculpture pieces. An account survives from the reign of the great Gupta emperor Samudra Gupta in A.D. 360 of the casting of an image of the Buddha

1

in gold and silver studded with gems. A similar incident was described in the reign of the king Harsha in the 7th century A.D.* The famous Chinese pilgrim Yuan Chwang who visited India during king Harsha's rule, wrote in his account of the return journey to his native land, that, " notwithstanding losses on more than one occasion, due to accident or robbery, he succeeded in bringing safely a hundred and fifty particles of Buddha's bodily relics; sundry images of the teacher in gold and silver and sandal wood, and no less than 657 volumes of manuscripts carried upon twenty horses." (V. A. Smith)

There is no vestige left of such gold or silver images as those described above. Metal images, especially those made in precious metals, had always been tempting loot to invading and victorious armies. Usually they were melted to provide cash and arms. But there are examples of later metal statuary—in copper, brass and bronze—from the medieval period onwards, both in North and South India. These can be grouped together to show the various techniques and styles evolved in Indian metal imagery.

II

Historical Outline.

For the history of Indian metal art, the country can be divided into three geographical parts:

1. Northern India or Hindusthan, comprising Sindh,

---

* " The centre of attraction was a great monastery and shrine specially erected upon the bank of the Ganges, where a golden image of Buddha equal to the king in stature, was kept in a tower 100 feet high. A similar but smaller image 3 feet in height was carried daily in solemn procession, escorted by twenty rajas and a train of three hundred elephants."—V. A. Smith.

the Punjab and the Gangetic plains, i.e., the lands lying between the Himalayan mountains and the Narbada river and Vindha hills.

2. The Deccan, which is the highlands lying between the Narbada river and the Tungabhadhra river.

3. The Far-South or the Tamil Land, which is the area between the Tungabhadhra river and Cape Comorin.

NORTHERN INDIA OR HINDUSTHAN

The earliest metal objects of art, except those found at the site of the Sindh-valley culture, belong to the time of the Imperial Gupta dynasty which ruled Hindusthan from the 4th century A.D. to the 6th century A.D. It is true that from the pre-Gupta period there survive some examples of gold, silver and bronze work with cast or repoussé human and animal figures. But their execution is unskilled and they clearly did not have any influence on the development of the statuaries of the later periods. On the other hand, the Gupta metal images have great artistic merit, though very few of them exist today. Moreover they show high technical skill in the casting of large-size figures. During this dynasty various classical traditions and foreign influences were completely blended and assimilated into the style of Indian figure art. At this time also the attitudes and gestures of the religious images became regulated by priestly codes. The style of sculpture formed by the Gupta artists became the ideal of art for later centuries and this continued until the practice of sculpture was abruptly ended by the advent of the Islamic armies which were pledged to the destruction of idols.

After the decline of the Gupta dynasty, North India suffered a period of anarchy and chaos which lasted nearly a century. At the beginning of the 7th century A.D. a king

3

named Harsha (A.D. 606—647), restored order and established himself as the imperial monarch of Hindusthan. He was a great king and like his predecessors, the Maurya King Asoka the great (298—273 B.C.), and the Kushan king Kanishka (A.D. 120—162), gave liberal patronage to Buddhism. Himself an accomplished poet and writer, king Harsha encouraged the practice of every kind of art and raised many monuments and shrines. There are ample records showing that during his rule, numerous large-size metal figures were made to adorn the palaces and temples. But hardly any sculpture of his time has survived.

After the death of king Harsha, Hindusthan was again plunged into incessant wars. The various territorial rulers fought one another for the vacant paramountcy. The strongest of these rulers were the Parihar Rajputs of Kanauj, the Pala kings of Bengal and Bihar, and Chandel kings of Jejakabhukti (the present-day Bundelkhand). There were many small kingdoms, mostly under Rajput princes, which joined in the fight with the greater powers. By turn each of the leading kings succeeded in gaining partial paramountcy over Hindusthan. While they enjoyed their brief authority, they built countless stone palaces and temples; these were lavishly decorated with paintings and sculptures. Although many of these palaces and temples still stand, the metal images and other art treasures which they housed have almost completely disappeared. Wars, foreign invasions, and the sacking of these buildings destroyed nearly all the examples of the metal art of the period. But we know that the sculpture of this time was of a very different style from that of the Gupta. It had lost the human quality of the earlier art: and its highly decorative patterns were made to harmonise with the architecture of the time.

4

A centre of special interest was Bengal and Bihar. There the Pala dynasty was a great patron of art, and under its rule North Indian metal statuary reached a new height. Two notable Pala kings Dharmapala and Devapala reigned for more than a century (A.D. 780—892) and during their rule literature and the fine arts greatly flourished. The Pala artists developed a very distinctive style which later strongly influenced the art of Nepal and Tibet.

Until the end of 10th century A.D., the Hindu kings of Northern India remained free to rule as they pleased and many of them indulged their tastes in raising grand edifices decorated with paintings and images. But from the 11th century A.D., the sporadic invasions by the Islamic army from the North-Western frontier shattered the structure of the Hindu kingdoms. These, weakened by the internal strife, were unable to put up any effective resistance. By the end of 12th century A.D., the Muslim chiefs had conquered the major part of Hindusthan and consolidated their power in establishing a strong rule which was to remain firm for some seven centuries. V. A. Smith, the famous writer on Indian history, wrote, " The more energetic Muslim sovereigns usually prided themselves on making as clean a sweep as possible of the buildings and art work of the Hindu idolaters, who had become their subjects. In pursuance of that policy during the course of five centuries (1200—1700), immense areas were absolutely denuded of all Hindu buildings and of course, at the same time, of all works of art connected with those buildings."

This more or less ended the practice of metal sculpture in Northern India. It is true that in the 16th and 17th century some of the Mogul rulers relaxed their restriction on Hindu religious ceremonial functions, and there were instances when metal images were made for temple and homes. But the creative genius of the old sculpture was lost irrevocably during the long suppression and wanton destruction of the art by the iconoclastic fanatics. Only in remote regions where the Islamic army could not penetrate, such as Nepal and Tibet, the practice of highly skilled metal statuary remained unhampered. There it is still very much alive today. And elsewhere also there has been a survival of the art in the making of toys and animal figures. For example in Rajputana and Bengal, it is possible to find human and animal figures which are reminiscences of the great metal art of the past.

THE DECCAN

The early history of the Deccan and of the far south of India is still very obscure. Except for the images found at Amaravati, the oldest surviving examples of Deccanese and South Indian metal statuaries cannot be dated before the 9th or 10th century A.D. But it would be wrong to suppose that the metal art of the Deccan and of the far south developed at a much later date than that of the north. There is much evidence to show that from very ancient time—preceding in fact the Mauryan king Asoka—the Deccan and the Far South had a highly developed civilization, independent of their northern neighbour. It was only from the beginning of the Christian era that the North Indian religion, philosophy, and Sanskrit language began to influence the Deccan and the Tamila-land.

The earliest known Imperial dynasty which ruled the Deccan was the Andhras and this was in power from the early 3rd century B.C. to the 3rd century A.D. No examples have come to light of Andhra metal sculpture. But there exist some magnificent Andhra stone sculptures whose prototypes might have been cast in metal. The history of the Deccan again becomes obscure between the decline of Andhra rule and the rise of the Chalukya dynasty which was founded by Pulakesin I in the middle of 6th century A.D. His son and successor Pulakesin II in the 7th century successfully resisted the attacks of king Harsha from the north and compelled him to acknowledge the river Narbada as the territorial boundary between their dominions. During the rule of this king, the Far South was divided between four important kingdoms—Pandya, Chera, Chola and Pallava, who were constantly at war with each other. The Pallavas and the Chalukyas also waged a war against each other which lasted for many years. In the end the sovereignty of the Deccan passed away to another dynasty—the Rashtrakutas in the middle of 8th century A.D. This dynasty remained in power for nearly two centuries and a half.

During the reign of the Chalukyas and the Rashtrakutas, many magnificent temples with excellent sculptures were raised all over the kingdom, and some of the finest cave temples were excavated during their rule. These are still fairly well preserved to this day. The Chalukyas were tolerant of all religious sects though they themselves were Brahmanical Hindus. Under the Rashtrakutas, Jainism enjoyed the principal state patronage. At the beginning of the 10th century A.D. the Chalukyas again re-established themselves in the southern Deccan by overthrowing the Rashtrakutas. But by this time the Chola dynasty had gained sovereignty over the other powers of the far Southern kingdoms and its northward expansion of empire brought it into conflict with the Chalukyas. While the Chalukyas and the Cholas were contesting for power, the Hoysalas of Mysore and the Yadavas of Devagiri, who were feudatory chieftains of the Chalukyas, established their independence. In the 12th century A.D. on the decline of the Chalukyas most of their possessions passed into the hands of these two new dynasties.

The great Hoysala king Bittideva or Bittiga, who later assumed the name of Vishnuvardhana after his conversion to the Vaishnava faith, erected temples of unique magnificence in which he installed many metal images of superb workmanship. Under the patronage of Vishnuvardhana and his successors there developed a splendid style in architecture and sculpture, whose characteristics can easily be distinguished from other Indian styles of art and buildings. But the history of sculpture in the Deccan was to end in the same way as in North India. In 14th century A.D. the Islamic forces of the north invaded the Deccan and completely overran the dominions of the Hoysalas and Yadavas, sacked their capital cities and reduced them to rubble.

FAR SOUTHERN INDIA OR TAMIL LAND.

The political and dynastic setting for the history of metal sculpture of far Southern India begins with the rise of the Cholas of the Vijayalaya line in the middle of the 9th century A.D. The earliest* surviving examples of metal statuary in the Tamil lands cannot be dated with certainty before the reign of the Chola king Rajaraja I at about the end of 10th century

*"The early works of art, executed in impermanent materials, have perished utterly and cannot be described. But beyond all doubt they existed in large numbers and were the foundation of more enduring works. The artists who designed the Pallava temples and wrought the sculptures on the rocks of Mamallapuram were not novices. They had served their apprenticeship, and when the call came to them to express their ideas in imperishable forms of stone they brought to bear on the new problem the skill acquired by generations of practice. The art of the Chola period is the continuation of that of Pallava times. No violent break separates the two stages. The changes which occurred took place gradually by a process of spontaneous development."—V. A. Smith: The Oxford History of India.

A.D. But the high standard of artistic skill, and perfection shown in the process of metal casting of the figures executed during this period must have been the result of a continuous practice and development of the art during many previous centuries.

The Chola kings Rajaraja-deva the great and his son Rajendra Chola-deva I, who ruled from A.D. 985 to 1035 were the most prominent sovereigns of the dynasty. The mighty army of these kings conquered vast territories in South India and the fleet of their powerful navy sailed far across the Bay of Bengal and the Indian Ocean and occupied Pegu in the East and Ceylon and other islands in the South sea. They were equally famous for building immense palaces and gigantic temples richly wrought with sculptures, and for excavating large artificial lakes, many of which are still fairly well preserved. The later Chola kings were involved in a prolonged conflict with the Chalukyas of the Deccan and in the middle of 10th century A.D. They were totally beaten by their adversaries. In A.D. 1074 Kulotunga Chola, who was an offspring of the Chola and Chalukya union, became the king of the Chola empire and enlarged his dominions by vast conquests. During his reign a large number of masterpieces of South Indian metal images were made, many of which have been preserved to this day. The Chola kings worshipped the god Siva and his consort Parvati. Some of the finest examples of metal sculptures of this period represent various aspects of these two divinities. They have been universally acclaimed as the flower of the artistic genius of South India.

The fall of Chola power in the 13th century A.D. brought about the decline in art, and particularly the art of metal sculpture. It was revived for a time by the last powerful

9

Hindu kings of Vijayanagar. The history of this dynasty is especially interesting.

In the 14th century A.D. the North Indian Islamic army invaded the Deccan and founded a Muslim state which soon threw off the suzerainty of the sultan of the north. Then it split up into a group of independent kingdoms. As a reaction to this Muslim intrusion five Hindu brothers who were either the fugitives from Warangal or chieftains under the Hoysala kings, founded the kingdom of Vijayanagar. It became involved in war with the neighbouring Muslim states and in its life of two centuries it knew no respite until it was at last conquered and destroyed. But in spite of the constant wars with the Muslim rulers, Vijayanagar flourished for a time in great splendour. The most noteworthy king of Vijayanagar was Krishna Deva Raya (1509—1529) under whose rule the kingdom excelled in wealth and culture. The building of many temples and palaces decorated with sculptures evolved a fine style in art and architecture. A large effigy in copper repoussé (Fig. 53) shows the king Krishna Deva Raya and his two queens. This reveals a very high degree of skill in beaten metal craft.

The end of Vijayanagar was tragic. In 1565 a confederated army of all the neighbouring Muslim kings attacked its ruler. Ram Raja, the minister of the king, who was virtually the real ruler, was felled and killed on the battlefield and following this the entire Hindu army was routed. The victorious Muslims lost no time in entering and sacking the capital city of Vijayanagar. " Nothing seemed to escape them. They broke up the pavilion standing on the huge platform from which the kings used to watch festivals and overthrew all carved work. They lit huge fires in the magnificently decorated buildings forming the temple of Vitthalaswami near the river and smashed its exquisite stone sculptures. With fire and sword, with crowbars and axes, they carried on day after day their work of destruction. Never perhaps in the history of the world has such havoc been wrought, wrought so suddenly, on so splendid a city teeming with a wealthy and industrious population in full plenitude of prosperity one day and on the next seized, pillaged, and reduced to ruins, amid scenes of savage massacre and horrors beggaring description." (Sewell)

Thus ended the last powerful Hindu kingdom and with it the creative genius of art and sculpture. The chiefs of various small states who survived the disaster of Vijayanagar, and the ruling princes of the far Southern territories who escaped the Muslim occupation continued to encourage the practice of art. But the productions of the post-Vijayanagar period, though they sometimes showed excellent skill and crafts-manship, were generally lacking in originality and expression.

III

The Ideals of Indian Figure Art.

From the examples of idols and images still extant, it is not really possible to reconstruct the development of Indian sculpture from its beginnings to the very high level which must have been reached before the period when the magnificent images which have survived were brought into being.

Indian sculpture, though comparatively young in age, has been often classed with the ancient arts of Egypt, Assyria and Greece. But it has neither the Egyptian's overwhelming manifestation of the spirit of the dead, nor the Greek's passionate admiration of the flesh and muscles of the living. Ancient Indian priests and poets described human emotions and actions metaphorically, and the artist, to express those

11

ideas, reconstructed the natural human and animal forms. A hero or a god was often described as having the powerful shoulders of a bull, a broad and strong chest like a pair of iron doors, the trim, slim waist of a lion and long powerful arms resembling the straight trunks of " Deodar " tree (like poplar). The artists, in creating the figure of a hero or a god, made a synthesis of these elements and produced an imaginative form in which these elements denoting his qualities could be identified. Thus the face of a goddess or heroine was compared with the beauty of the full moon or lotus, her soft and delicate arms with the creepers, the long, tapering fingers with the tendrils, the fullness of bosom and the slenderness of her waist with the flowering tree, the trunk of which is bent by the weight of the full blossom, her shapely legs with the smooth and round trunk of the banana tree and her small feet with the leaves of a sapling.

This ideal of the harmonious embodiment of nature in human form did not result from an aversion of the sculptor from flesh or from the natural sensuous appeal in the human figure. It was adopted deliberately in an attempt to fuse the material form with the spiritual and cosmic world. With every aspect of human emotion translated into an aesthetic order, there was very little vulgarity in Indian sculpture. Even the representation of erotic subjects in some periods of Indian figure art was not attempted for sensual reasons: they only provided excellent sculptural opportunities.

In Indian figure art every character, whether high or low, was most carefully symbolised. The qualities which distinguish the god from a demon, the wise from the ignorant, are interpreted in an idiom which contains different signs and symbols to explain each character. In Indian iconography, human forms were shown in various conventional patterns with many adjunctive signs and symbols to denote abstract and infinite qualities. Though the naturalistic representation of the human figure was partially disregarded, the unity of the limbs and the basic proportion of the body were rarely distorted. The interpretation of abstract concepts in concrete form sometimes produced elaborate structures, but their accomplishment in neat sculptural forms is almost unparalleled.

The symbols and images in Indian art will not appear so complex if one understands the religious or the philosophical ideas they portray. The image of the Buddha is not merely a figure of a yogi meditating, but it symbolises the divine wisdom which the Buddha attained by his austerity and meditation. Whether standing or seated the image of the Buddha depicts perpetual bliss and timeless equilibrium amidst chaos. (Figs. 30, 31.)

In the magnificent bronze figure of Nataraja (Figs. 28, 50) the sculptor did not try to mould the image of a dancer or show the style of dance. He aimed at representing the joy of victory which the great Siva might have experienced in his cosmic dance. There is an intrinsic value in each component of the robe, headdress, and the gesture of the hands of these figures. In general, Indian sculptures are integrally connected with the architecture of the monasteries, temples, monumental gateways and palaces. The metal figures were in most cases portable in order that they might be carried in ceremonial processions. They had also a close relationship with the setting of the galleries and niches of the shrines in which they repose. Furthermore, the artist often contorted the form of the human and animal figures to harmonise them with the architecture or to fit into the shape of the recesses of the walls. But these exaggerated and humanly impossible attitudes of the figures are so carefully balanced and their patterns are so complete that they do not appear as unnatural or grotesque. Anyone who is not familiar with Indian mythology and literature may easily be confused when confronted with the many-headed and multi-armed figures. Apart from religious significance, the multiplicity of heads and arms represents the magnitude of the power of which these personalities—gods or demons—are supposed to possess.

The material and method used in sculpture have limitations in depicting the effect of movements such as flying in the air or floating on water. Attempts to translate motion in stone or metal do not ordinarily produce a very successful impression of continuous movement, even when outstretched wings and fins are attached to the human figures. But the Indian sculptors made it clear that the human forms (representing heavenly minstrels and dancers and divinities) were flying and floating without needing to give them wings or fins attached to their bodies. The figures of Gandharvas and Apsaras can clearly be seen as gliding along in the sky. The dancing Sivas and Krishnas, with the rhythmic swing of their arms, robes and ornaments, transmit an endless vibrant motion even through its vehicle of stone and metal. (Figs. 31, 38, 59.)

The most outstanding feature of Indian imagery is that since the days when the priests and iconographers prescribed the types and attributive signs of divinities and demoniac or spiritual characters, the sculptors were only allowed to interpret those fixed descriptions of images without omitting or changing any detail of the set patterns. And yet under such rigorous suppression of self-interpretation the Indian sculptors have produced magnificent sculptures. In all

14

probability many of the outstanding works were collective efforts guided by one master. Such examples show that the group of artists working on the same figure had such similar ideas that the result they produced appeared to be the work of one sculptor.

There are practically no portrait sculptures in Indian figure-art. It is true that there are many metal images of royal personages and donors, but they are really effigies rather than portraits in the strict sense of the word. They usually show authentic contemporary costumes and other details, but their features show rather the common racial types than individualised likenesses.

IV

Indian Iconometry

There are no definite indications that the human form was represented in art in Vedic times. It is true that the references to decorations and jewelries in the Vedas may suggest that human and animal forms were incorporated in the designs of the metal ornaments. But there is not enough evidence to prove that there was anthropomorphic representation of the Vedic gods. In the stone sculptures of later times, during the Maurya, Sunga and Kushan dynasties which ruled North India from the 3rd century B.C. to the beginning of the 3rd century A.D., the gods and demi-gods were represented as ordinary human beings, and their attitudes and gestures were restricted to conventional symbolical positions and movements. But in these earliest examples of Indian sculptures the practice of suppressing superfluous anatomical details in both human and animal forms was apparent.

Various treatises exist on image-making, most of them

written during and after Gupta rule. The rules and regulations laid down by these Silpa-sastras (or art treatises) had to be strictly followed by the artists of the later periods; and although as time went by the contents of the books were elaborated, the fundamentals of Gupta art theory have remained unchanged in India up to today. South Indian sculptures, though differing considerably in style and workmanship from the northern types, followed the basic priestly codes of the north in all that concerned the attitudes and gestures of the images.

The Indian images are of two types, static and dynamic. Posture could be standing, sitting or reclining. Images can be broadly grouped into four types according to their attitudes. They are: *Samabhanga* or *Samapada*, *Abhanga*, *Tribhanga* and *Atibhanga*.

Samabhanga or *Samapada*: In this attitude the left and right halves of the figure are shown in symmetrical patterns. Whether standing or seated the figure is poised more or less perpendicular to its pedestal without inclining to the right or left. (Figs. 5, 8, 9, 19, 33, 34, 39.)

Abhanga: In this attitude the upper half of the figure is inclined slightly to the right or left without changing very much the Samapada position of the lower half of the body. (Figs. 4, 28, 36, 40.)

Tribhanga: In this attitude the lower limbs up to the hips are inclined to the right and the trunk and shoulder to the left while the neck and head lean to the right, or the reverse arrangement of the same. (Fig. 31.)

Atibhanga : In this attitude the Tribhanga pose is very much emphasised. The upper half of the body from the hips is bent in a sweeping curve to the right or left, backwards or forwards. The lower limbs are also bent or stretched sideways or backwards or forwards to show dynamic movement.

The figures of the post-Gupta period usually show slim and trim bodies, but there are also thin and fat figures made specifically to represent certain characters. In one of the ancient Indian art treatises it is mentioned that " an emaciated image brings famine, a stout image spells sickness for all, while one that is well proportioned, without displaying any bones, muscles or veins, will always enhance one's prosperity."* These regulations resulted in the creation of a very conventional bodily form which was commonly used in idols. But characters which were neither gods nor goddesses were exempted from the requisites of the religious codes. The artists were free to design them according to their own ideas. Thus we have flying angels and demi-gods described as the *Ganas, Gandharvas, Vidyadharas, Apsaras*, etc., as well as the water and tree nymphs. But these figures were in most cases integrally connected with the main subject of the sculpture. To maintain balance and harmony of the plastic pattern, they were given more or less the same conventional physical build laid down by the religious text-book. It was only in representing animal figures in sculpture that the Indian artists allowed themselves complete freedom of self-expression.

The devices of dwarfing and enlarging the size and volume of figures were used in Indian sculpture to denote the greater and lesser, or the more powerful and the less powerful, heroes, gods, and demons. Comparative measurements were laid down for the respective images in their various aspects. The unit measure used in Indian iconography is called *Tala*: "A quarter of the width of the artist's own first is called an *Angula* or finger's width. Twelve such finger widths is the

Artistic Anatomy, by A. N. Tagore.

17

measure of a tala " (A. N. Tagore). The human figure and the gods in their calmer and pleasanter aspects measured ten talas. But when they were performing heroic actions, this height was increased to twelve talas; in their fierce and demonic aspects they were given a height of fourteen talas. Goddesses were restricted to the height of nine tala measure, and child figures measured six talas. There are exceptions to these rules. Measurements differ in the north and south of India, and also vary in special gods, goddesses and demons.

Various seated poses of the Indian images were prescribed by many treatises on iconography. " The principal seated poses are the *Padmasana* (also known as *Paryankasana*), typically seen in the seated Buddha, where the legs are crossed and each foot rests on the opposite thigh; in *Virasana*, the pose is similar, but the right foot lies under instead of upon the left thigh; the *Yogasana*, the legs being similarly crossed, the knees slightly raised and supported by a narrow band called *Yoga-patta*; *Sukhasana*, *Lalitasana*, *Lalitaksepa* or *Lilaksepa*, a position of ease or comfort, where one leg remains bent, the other is pendent; *Sopasryasana*, when the raised knees are supported by a Yoga-patta; *Maharaja-lilasana*, ' position of royal pleasure,' where one knee remains bent in the same way, but the other is raised and supports the corresponding arm, the hand hanging over the knee, the body leaning slightly backward and supported by the other arm. Figures seated in the European manner (*Pralamabapada asana*) are less usual, except in the case of *Maitreya Bodhisattva*; even for Buddhas this type is comparatively rare, and it is not found in Brahmonical art." (A. K. Coomaraswamy)

The symbolical hand gestures of images which are called *Mudra* or *Hasta* were also prescribed by the old scriptures on Indian imagery. The following are the usual hand gestures found in Indian images:

Dhayana or *Yoga mudra* signifies the gesture of meditation. This shows one hand resting on the other in the lap of a figure seated in Padma or Paryanka asana. (Figs. 33, 34.)

Varda or *Vara mudra* represents charity and shows the open palm held outwards and the fingers pointed downwards. (Figs. 4, 10 right hand.)

Abhaya mudra or the gesture of assurance (do not fear) shows the open palm held outwards, the extended fingers directed upwards. (Fig. 30 lower right hand.)

Vyakhyana mudra means exposition which is shown by holding the hand in the same position as in Abhaya mudra, but the thumb and forefinger touching. (Figs. 10, 11 left hand, 45 right hand.)

Dhramachakra mudra signifies the " Wheel of the Law," i.e., the first preaching of the Buddha which shows both hands held before the chest, the right in Vyakhyana mudra, and the left with palm inwards. (Fig. 8.)

Anjali hasta shows the hands folded palm to palm in reverence. (Figs. 39, 53.)

Kataka hasta (or *Simha Karna*) shows the hands partly closed, the index and middle fingers almost touching the thumb. This gesture usually signifies that the hand is holding attributes or the stem of flowers. (Figs. 52 right hand, 48 lower left hand.)

Kartari Mukha hasta shows the thumb and the third finger being bent are in near contact, and other fingers are outstretched and separated in holding attributes. (Fig. 48 upper left and right hands.)

Suchi hasta is almost similar as the Kataka, but with the index finger raised in pointing or threatening. (Fig. 38 right hand.)

V

CHART SHOWING THE MAIN SCHOOLS OF SCULPTURE

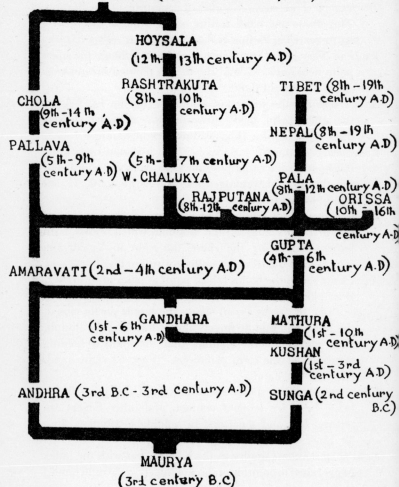

VIJAYANAGAR (14th – 17th century A.D)

HOYSALA
(12th – 13th century A.D)

RASHTRAKUTA
(8th – 10th
century A.D)

TIBET (8th – 19th
century A.D)

CHOLA
(9th – 14th
century A.D)

NEPAL (8th – 19th
century A.D)

PALLAVA
(5th – 9th
century A.D)

(5th – 7th century A.D)
W. CHALUKYA

PALA
(8th – 12th century A.D)

RAJPUTANA
(8th – 12th century A.D)

ORISSA
(10th – 16th
century A.D)

GUPTA
(4th – 6th
century A.D)

AMARAVATI (2nd – 4th century A.D)

(1st – 6th) GANDHARA
century A.D)

MATHURA
(1st – 10th
century A.D)

KUSHAN
(1st – 3rd
century A.D)

ANDHRA (3rd B.C – 3rd century A.D)

SUNGA (2nd century
B.C)

MAURYA
(3rd century B.C)

VI

Styles and Schools of Metal Sculpture.

There is historical evidence that whenever a strong ruling dynasty established its sway over a large dominion in India, the intellectual and artistic genius was stimulated, and produced remarkable works of art. The different styles in Indian metal sculpture were all evolved as the result of the rise of powerful dynasties. The earliest style in metal statuary is that of the Guptas: at least no earlier examples of metal sculpture of note have been found preceding their time. " The art of casting copper statues on a large scale by the *cire perdue* process was practised with considerable success. A copper image of Buddha about 80 feet high was erected at Nalanda in Bihar at the close of the sixth century; and the fine Sultanganj Buddha, 7½ feet is still to be seen in the museum at Birmingham." (V. A. Smith)*

THE GUPTA STYLE (A.D. 320—490)

In Gupta sculpture all anthropomorphic figures of the divinities were given slim bodies and extremely diaphanous robes which clung to the limbs and thus revealed their form. The rendering of the hair—especially of the male heads— was conventionalised; the hair looks like a wig rather than a natural coiffure. In many of the Gupta figures the inter-spaces between the fingers of the hands were blocked up, and this gave the appearance of webbed fingers. The human and naturalistic qualities of the sculptures of the older schools of Maurya and Kushan dynasties were retained by the Gupta artists though the images were rapidly assuming hieratic

*See Fig. 85 in *Classical Indian Sculpture*, by the author.

forms. The kindly spirit of Buddhism profoundly influenced the art of North India, and even the gradual decline of Buddhism and the rise of the Brahmanic faith in the post-Gupta periods did very little to alter the pleasant and compassionate bearing of the images. Although many of the Gupta images have extra arms and heads according to the ritual prescriptions, they look thoroughly human beings who can share love and joy with the mortals. The freshness, grace and vitality of the Gupta sculpture have rarely been surpassed by other schools of Indian figure-art.

THE PALA SCHOOL (A.D. 750—1200)

The next main style in metal sculpture of the north was developed during the rule of the Pala dynasty of Bengal and Bihar. There may have been a strong growth of important metal sculpture in king Harshavardhan's reign, for there are epigraphical references; but no concrete examples so far have been found. In the Pala period there was a revival of Buddhist images though they were very much mixed up with the Brahmanic iconography. The Pala images retained the slim and trim bodily forms of the Gupta style but the diaphanous robe became scantier, and except for the parts covered by the elaborate jewelries the body above the waist was shown in the nude. The attitude became formal and highly conventionalised. Faces were given sharp, aquiline noses and half-shut eyes denoting meditation. The eyebrows and mouth were clearly defined by finely chased ridges. The Pala artists produced many group figures in metal comprising two or more figures on one pedestal. But as a whole the Pala sculptures lack the human spirit and vitality of the Gupta images.

There is a record of two very eminent artists of the Pala period, named Dhiman and his son Bitopala, who were experts in sculpture and painting and produced many images in cast metal during the rule of Devapala in 9th century A.D. A distinct school rose following their works which gained reputation as the sculptures of the Eastern style. The Pala sculpture influenced the art of Nepal and Tibet in the Himalayan regions and also the art of Orissa in the south.

NEPAL

Indian metal sculpture probably reached Nepal during the Gupta rule and was certainly known in king Harsha's time. The earlier works of Nepalese sculpture show the classical tradition of the Gupta art. In the 7th and 8th century A.D. the Indian imagery went to Tibet through Nepal which became more or less dependent on Tibet. Since then the art of metal statuary in these regions (being unaffected by the Islamic encroachment) has continued to flourish and it is still practised down to the present times. The early Nepalese and Tibetan images were close to the tradition of Bengali sculpture. The idols made in Nepal and Tibet are mostly in beaten copper as well as cast in brass, though there exist some examples of the early period cast in bronze. The images are usually decorated with gilt and set with rubies, turquoise, lapislazuli and crystals; they conceal the cold surface of metal and envelop the figures with warmth and colour.

Dr. Coomaraswamy gave a very fine description on the style of Nepalese sculpture. " In the older Nepalese figures, the Indian character is altogether predominant, and there is no suggestion whatever of anything Mongolian : they recall the work of the Gupta period, and are, perhaps, as near as we can hope to get examples of Taranatha's ' School of the East,' and they cannot be wholly unrelated to the works of the Bengali school of Dhiman and Bitpalo. They are characterized by a very full modelling of the flesh and almost florid features: the bridge of the nose is markedly rounded and the lips full. On the other hand, those of a later date, and up to modern times, are no longer so robust and fleshy, but svelte and slender-waisted and more sharply contoured: the nose becomes aquiline, sometimes even hooked, the lips clear-cut and thin, and the expression almost arch. Thus the development involves attention and refinement of form: at the same time, iconographically speaking, the forms are often much more complicated and the ornament richer. To sum up these distinctions the art of the earlier figures is plastic and sculpturesque, while that of the latter has more the character of drawing and suggests the hand of the goldsmith rather than a modeller." (*Rupam*, vol. 2)

TIBET

Tibetan sculpture developed in the Indian tradition through the agency of the Nepalese school. It was also partly influenced by China. It is true that the Buddhist images of China themselves reveal the influence of the orthodox style of the Gupta school and the Graeco-Indian style of the Gandhara school. In China the characteristic heavily folded drapery of the Gandhara sculpture became thinner and decorative; this was perhaps to harmonise with the Indian forms of the images which became known through the importation of Indian idols, as well as through the Indian artists who worked in China.* Tibet was closely

*" A Nepalese artist by the name, according to Chinese transcription, of Ar-ni-ko, a draughtsman, painter, sculptor and decorator, and accustomed to repeat the Canon of Proportions, and excelling in designing, moulding and casting images, was invited in the thirteenth century to the court of the Chinese Emperor and had there a very high reputation. His Canon of Proportions, attributed, like the Sinhalese canon, to Sariputra, was translated into Chinese in the 17th century, and was printed in Japan in 1885."—(Rupam No. 6. April, 1921.)

connected with China for many centuries. Some of the characteristics of this hybrid Gandharan-Chinese and Indian sculpture, specially the style of the drapery, was thus introduced into the figure-art of Tibet.

Examples of metal figures of the Andhra and Chalukya periods are very rare. But they shared probably the same characteristics as the stone sculptures of this period. On this assumption the surviving stone sculptures of the Andhra and Chalukya school deserve a brief description.

The most notable monuments containing Andhra sculptures are the magnificent gates of the Sanchi Stupa and the Stupa of Amaravati. Of these the sculptures of Amaravati are the more important in their bearing on the development of figure-art in the South. Some bronze figures found at the site of Amaravati show that the art of metal statuary was thriving in the 3rd century A.D. The stone sculptures of the Stupa seem to have developed by various stages: from the Mauryan and Sunga archaic types to the Graeco-Indian style of Gandhara and the indigenous powerful figures of the Kushan Mathura.

The Chalukyan empire in the Deccan stretched from the East to the West coast of the sea and for the convenience of administration was divided into two kingdoms. The Western Chalukyan sculptures, most of which are in stone, show very strong Gupta influence. The early Tamil sculpture, though contemporaneous with the early Chalukyan art, displays an independent style influenced partly by the Amaravati tradition. Very little is known about the art practised in the Eastern Chalukyan empire. The Rashtrakutas who succeeded the Western Chalukyas continued the tradition of their predecessors.

The distinctive styles of sculpture of the Tamil land, which mainly developed locally, can be grouped under the following heads: *Pallavas, Early Cholas, Late Chola* and *Vijayanagar.* It is still very difficult to ascertain the age of most of the South Indian metal figures. There are of course some examples with inscribed dates and legends. The approximate dates of the uninscribed images have been guessed by various experts by their similarities to stone figures which fortunately can be fairly correctly dated.

Many metal figures of the dancing Siva have been ascribed to the Pallava period by some scholars. But a reliable history of the South Indian metal statuary begins only with the Chola period.*

Chola metal sculptures exist in considerable numbers. Most of them are of individual figures, but there exist also group figures of a husband and wife, a brother and sister, a father and son, a king with his heir-apparent or queen, as well as a god with his consort and offspring, and sometimes coupled with their devotees. But these, although fashioned on the same pedestal, are in most cases really an assemblage of individual figures and they could be separated from each other without breaking the harmony. Most of the Chola sculptures, which represent gods, are of various aspects of the god Siva and his consort Parvati and their son the war god Skanda. There are many quasi-portrait sculptures of various Chola rulers and their queens, the Saivaite and

*The Pallava stone sculptures show a naturalistic pose and unconventional attitudes. The human faces are elongated and have a broad nose, full lips and double-chin. The body shows massive archaic form without much anatomical shape. The drapery is over-simplified and rarely indicates the details of the folds. The group sculptures, many of which were hewn out of the original rock, display excellent natural movement and monumental quality.

Vaishnavaite saints and the donors which are in most cases inscribed with the name of the person they are supposed to represent. There is also another class of sculpture—human figures holding a lamp; this holds a unique position in South Indian imagery. " These lamps or Deepas are of two kinds —those which were used for the ceremony of Arati (the waving of the lamp) and those that were kept burning before the images throughout the nights, as a symbol, as it were, of the burning devotion of the donor. Many of these lamps were artistically conceived in the form of a female figure holding the burner, the donor of the gift being suggested by the figure. These are now known as the Dipa-Lakshmis or ' beauty-lamps ' and they inspired the South Indian bronze workers to produce some finest pieces of sculpture." (O. C. Gangoly, *South Indian Bronzes*) (Figs. 13, 19, 21, 22.)

The Chola figures show much more natural roundness of the human body than the Pallava sculptures, and although the attitudes are formal and the gestures are conventional they express dignity and vitality. The Chola faces are smooth and round-shaped, decorations are simple; the necklaces are in broad designs and are arranged in circular pattern round the neck. They rarely hang down between the breasts or are bent into ornate patterns. The figures usually wear a bangle immediately above the elbow, a part of which some-times projects from the outer side of the arm. The girdles round the waist of the figures are in most cases very realistically shaped with a gorgon-like head in the front for the buckle and with long festoons hanging down. (Figs. 39, 40, 41.)

In the later Chola style the figures assumed more conven-tional attitudes, standing or seated in stiff attention. The nose became more pronounced and the torso was modelled to show robustness and power.

The Hoysala and Yadava sculptures have a special place in the South Indian figure-art for their very florid and decorative style deriving their main elements from the Western Chalukyan sculptures. The Chalukya and Chola art, which for centuries developed side by side more or less independently of each other, were finally merged in the sculptures of Vijayanagar. The figures in this style look very formal and have little appearance of modelling. The draperies are shaped in elaborate conventional patterns. The faces are expressionless except for the widely shaped eyes which have a perpetual stare. The nose was fashioned with a sharp prominence and the chin with a vertical groove. The abdomen usually is emphatically round and somewhat drooping forwards. The navel is in most cases shown with ray-like horizontal and vertical lines.

The metal images of the post-Vijayanagar periods show very little life and vigour compared with earlier work, and their workmanship is usually much less refined. The South Indian metal statuary of the late periods, which has been continued almost up to the present time, exhibits mainly a decadent Vijayanagar style.

VII

The Technique of Metal Statuary in India.

It has already been stated that most of the examples of metal figures which exist today, are of pure copper or copper-base alloys and brass. The scarcity of the bronze images (as the metal is commonly understood) may have been due to the fact that tin was not easy to get in the quantity required for the alloy. There may be another reason for not using the common bronze; according to the Hindu religious ideas this alloy was considered as impure for divine rites. From very early periods various metals were considered to symbolise different stars; and in the making of images particular metals were selected in the amalgam to signify the cosmic relation of the idol. In the north the amalgam of eight metals known as *Astadhatu*, which is composed of gold, silver, iron, tin, lead, mercury, copper and zinc, was considered as the most perfect and prized alloy for the making of divine images. In South India the ideal alloy for statuary has always been the " Pancha Lauha." This literally means the five irons, but is in fact an amalgam of copper, silver, gold, brass and white lead. The casting of images in brass has been carried on both in North and South India since the 10th century A.D.

Almost all the images of the early periods show delicate modelling, and although the details of the bones and muscles were suppressed in the simplified forms they have the grace of the natural human body. But in the works of the later periods, the figures were most diligently chased out and this obliterated the tactile beauty of the sculptures. The modelling was completely overpowered by the hammering and engraving of the craftsman. The images look like the handiwork of the goldsmith rather than of the sculptor. Sometimes the figures were carved and engraved in the wax and after the casting in metal their details were emphasised by chasing.

The methods of casting metal figures in the Gupta period can be investigated by examining the colossal copper image of the Buddha from Sultanganj which is now in the Museum and Art Gallery, Birmingham. This seems to have been made in two layers. The inner layer was moulded on a core made of a mixture of sand, clay, charcoal and rice-husks. The segments of the layer were supported by iron rods of nearly three-quarters of an inch thick. The outer layer of copper was cast on the inner one by the *cire perdue* process and was made in several sections.

There are various references to the process of *cire perdue* in some of the ancient religious manuscripts, and in Manasara —an ancient text-book on image-making—there is a fairly detailed description of this process as it was practised in the old times. This is worth quoting at some length.

"According to the navatala measurement as mentioned before, the expert should first prepare the image (i.e., the mould), complete with all the limbs, yellowish in colour, beautiful to look at and with weapons and arms as prescribed.

After placing the wax tubes of the length of a ' dhatura ' flower on the back, on the shoulders and on the neck or the crown (of the image), (the artist) should besmear the image with refined clay.

To clay should be added charred husk finely rubbed, cotton severed a hundred times and a little salt finely powdered. All these (when mixed with clay) should be (finely) ground on a smooth stone and (the paste) should be applied three times all over and round (the image).

The first layer (of clay) should be transparent (and thin) and should be dried up in shade. After a couple of days a second layer should again (be applied). When dry again, there should be the third coating thickly applied.

(One) should besmear the whole (image or model) with clay leaving the mouths of the tubes open; and the wise man should dry up (the clay coating) with care and judgment.

The expert should first (i.e., before beginning the process, just mentioned) measure the wax of the image, which has to be made either in brass, or copper, or silver or gold.

Brass and copper should be taken ten times that of wax, silver twelve times and gold sixteen.

(Then one) should encase the metal, either gold or one that is desired, with clay and coconut-shaped crucible (thus formed) should be dried up in the aforesaid manner.

Next (one) should melt away the wax (from the mould) by heating the (i.e., the mould) in fire and should afterwards heat the crucible in cinders.

Brass and copper melt surely with (the help of) cinders just kindled. Silver melts with (the help of) glowing cinders, while gold with (the help of) cinders flaming fivefold.

After making a hole with an iron on the top of the crucible and holding it tightly with a pair of tongs (one) should bring the heated crucible (out of the cinders).

(One) should place a burning wick in the mouth of the tube of the heated (mould of the) image.

After bending carefully the crucible, held tightly by the tongs, (one) should pour molten metal into the mouth of the tube in a continuous stream and stop when it is full to the brim of the tube.

The adjacent fire should be put out for the purpose of cooling (the mould with the molten metal). When the image (i.e., the mould) gets naturally cool the expert should break up the clay (mould) very carefully.

Then the metal image (thus prepared) verily resembles that in wax, endowed with similar limbs and other details.

When there is seen anything superfluous that should be put right with ' charana '; the tubes should also be cut away and after that (the image) would have to be finished.

After making an image by this method, the king should install it on an auspicious day according to the usual rites and should offer daily worship to it." *

The text of Manasara advises that wax models should be made in yellowish colour, that being the nearest to the colour of the metals generally used for statuary except silver. It would thus ensure right modelling and the display of light and shadow to the final cast.

The process of metal-casting in the manner described in Manasara is still carried out in Nepal and in some parts of South India. The tools used by the Indian experts for metal statuary differ very little from those which are employed for the woodwork or stone-carving.

*An ancient text on the metal casting of metal images, by Sarasi kumar Saraswati. Journal of The Indian Society of Oriental Art, 1936.

According to the Indian tradition an artist is only considered accomplished when his repertoire of art consists of works in ten different materials. These are wood, brick (terra-cotta), stone, lime (stucco), plaster, sugar, ivory, Yantra(?), and flat drawing and painting. This versatile technical skill of the Indian artist is unique and is visibly present in the neat and complete workmanship which is found even in decadent art.

VIII

Short Chronology of Indian History.

NORTH INDIA

Indus Valley Culture,	c. 2500—1650 B.C.
Aryan Invasions of Northern India, (Vedic and Epic periods)	2000—1000 B.C.
Early Dynasties,	650—322 B.C.
Gautama Buddha,	563—483 B.C.
Mahavira, founder of the Jain Faith,	550—477 B.C.
Maurya Dynasty,	322—185 B.C.
Chandragupta	(322—298 B.C.)
Asoka	(273—232 B.C.)

Early stone monuments and sculptures.

Sunga and Kanva Dynasties,	185—28 B.C.

Stone monuments and sculptures.

Invasion of Alexander the Great,	327—325 B.C.
Indo-Greek and Indo-Parthian Dynasties	250 B.C.—A.D. 48

Rise of the Gandhara or Indo-Greek School of Sculpture.

Kushan Dynasty, A.D. 48—250
   School of Sculpture at Mathura. First Appearance of the Buddha image.

Imperial Guptas, A.D. 320—490
   Golden age of Indian sculpture.

Hashavardhan, King of Kanauj, A.D. 606—647

Solanki Dynasty of Gujrat, A.D. 765—1197
   Highly decorative sculptures of Jain temples at Mount Abu, Girnar and Satrunjaya.

Pala and Sena Dynasties of Bengal, A.D. 750—1200
   Metal and stone sculptures.

Rajput Dynasties of Central India, A.D. 816—1180
   Sculptured temples at Khajraho.

Ganga kingdom of Orissa, A.D. 1076—1586

Anantavarman Choda Ganga, A.D. 1076—1148
   Temple of Jagannath at Puri.

Solar Dynasty, A.D. 1434—1586
   Sculptured temple at Konarak and Bhuvaneswar.

Sultanate of Delhi, A.D. 1296—1526

Muslim kingdoms of Bengal, Gujrat and the Deccan—

The Mughal Empire, A.D. 1526—1857

Sikh kingdom of the Punjab, A.D. 1790—1849

British Period, A.D. 1857—1946

THE DECCAN

The Andhra Dynasty, 230 B.C.—A.D. 225
   Cave temples, sculptured stupas at Amaravati and Nagarjunikonda. Best paintings at Ajanta cave temples.

Chalukya Dynasty, A.D. 550—642
   Sculptured cave temples of Ellora.

Rashtrakuta Dynasty,   A.D. 757—973
    Kailasha temple at Ellora, and temples at Badami.

Ganga, Hoysala and Yadava Dynasties
    of Mysore,   A.D. 1111—1318
    Monumental Jain statues and sculptured temples at
    Halebid and Belur.

Muslim rulers of Bahmoni, and Adil Shahi
    Dynasties and the kings of Bijapur,   A.D. 1347—1673

Kingdom of Vijayanagar,   A.D. 1336—1646

Maratha Power,   A.D. 1670—1818

FAR SOUTHERN INDIA

The Pallava Dynasty,   A.D. 600—750
    Rock-cut temples at Mamallapuram and sculptured
    effigies of Pallava kings.

Chola Dynasty,   A.D. 907—1053
    Sculptured temples at Tanjore and Madura.

Pandya Dynasty,   A.D. 1251—1310

BIBLIOGRAPHY

ARAVAMUTHAN, T. G. *Portrait Sculpture in South India*; London, 1931.

BIRDWOOD, SIR GEORGE C. M. *The Industrial Arts of India*; London, 1880.

CHANDA, R. P. *Eastern Indian School of Mediaeval Sculpture, Archaeological Survey of India*; New Imperial Series, Vol. XLVII, 1933.

COOMARASWAMY, A. K. *Catalogue of the Indian Collections in the Museum of Fine Arts*; Boston, 1925.
History of Indian and Indonesian Art; London, 1927.
The Arts and Crafts of India and Ceylon; London, 1913.

GANGOLY, O. C. *South Indian Bronzes*; Calcutta, 1915.

GRAVELY, F. and RAMACHANDRAN, T. N. *Catalogue of South Indian Hindu Metal Images in the Madras Museum. Madras Museum Bulletin*; New Series. Vol., pt., 1932.

HAVELL, E. B. *Indian Sculpture and Painting*; London, 1908. (1st edition)

RAO, T. A. GOPINATHA *Elements of Hindu Iconography*; Madras, 1916.

SASTRI, H. K. *South Indian Gods and Goddesses*; Madras, 1916.

SEWELL, A. *A forgotten empire*; London, 1900.

SMITH, V. A. *History of Fine Art in India and Ceylon*; Oxford, 1911.
Oxford History of India; Oxford, 1920.
Sculpture of the Gupta Period, Ostasiatische Neitschrift. Vol. III, 1915.

TAGORE, A. N. *Some Notes on Indian Artistic Anatomy*; Calcutta, 1914.

DESCRIPTIVE NOTES TO PLATES

(The illustrations are arranged chronologically as far as possible in three groups showing the examples from North India, the Deccan and the Far South.)

1. YOUNG COUPLE. Gold repoussé, lac filled. Height 4.5cm. Provenance: Sirkap, Taxila, West Punjab. *Now at Central Asian Antiquities Museum, New Delhi.* Early 1st century A.D. *Photo: courtesy, Royal Academy of Arts, London.*

   The figures show delicate modelling. The soft effect of the original wax model is not obliterated by chasing. Compared with the typical metal statuary of the Indian mainland this example of the Gandhara school shows a very different style and expression.

2. BULL. Bronze. Height 5½ inches. Provenance: Sahri-Bahol, Gandhara. *Now in the Indian Section, Victoria and Albert Museum, London.* 3rd—4th century A.D. *Photo: author.*

   The animal is of typical Indian breed. Compared with the bull illustrated in plate No. 61, this example shows little vitality and movement.

3. BRAHMA. Bronze gilt and inlaid with copper. Height 109cm. Provenance: Mirpurkhas, Sind. *Now at Victoria Museum, Karachi.* 6th century A.D. *Photo: courtesy, Royal Academy of Arts, London.*

   The figure represents the divinity of creation. Its four heads signify the four cardinal points. The braided, piled-high hair and the meditative expression of the face are that of a yogi. The modelling of the upper half of the figure is naturalistic and monumental. A stag skin is seen hanging down from its left shoulder and the *Dhoti* it is wearing from the waist below is extremely diaphanous and reveals the form. The legs and feet are less naturalistic and stiff. The hand gestures are unusual in the iconography of the post-Gupta period but graceful and expressive.

4. AVALOKITESVARA. Copper gilt and jewelled with jacinth. Height 30.5cm. Provenance: Nepal. *Now at Museum of Fine Arts, Boston.* 9th-10th century A.D. *Photo: courtesy, Museum of Fine Arts, Boston.*

   The figure stands in slightly broken *Abhanga* pose. Though very much chased the face and body show traces of delicate modelling. The conventional decorative robe is well balanced with the movement and pattern of the figure. The right-hand gesture signifies charity and the left hand holds the stem of a rose-lotus which rests against the left shoulder.

5. BALARAMA, LAKSHMI AND VASUDEVA. Bronze. Height 11½ inches. Provenance: Bengal. *Now at British Museum, London.* Dedicated in the 48th year of King Mahipala, A.D. 1040. *Photo: courtesy, British Museum, London.*

The figures are standing in *Samapada* attitude, somewhat stiff and conventional in their execution.

6. SIVA AND UMA. Brass. Height 16cm. Provenance: Bengal. *Now at Museum of Fine Arts, Boston.* 10th—11th century A.D. *Photo: courtesy, Museum of Fine Arts, Boston.*

This is an excellent example of Pala sculpture. Though badly corroded the composition shows a compact pattern arranged skilfully in which the limbs of the two figures are artistically interlaced.

7. LOKULISHA (?). Copper gilt. Height 8 inches. Provenance: unknown, probably Bihar. *Now in the Indian Section, Victoria and Albert Museum, London.* 9th—10th century A.D. *Photo: author.*

The figure is seated in *Yogasana* pose with its hands resting on the knees. The matted locks are shown piled up over the royal crown. The face expresses deep meditation.

8. PRAJNAPARAMITA (?). Copper gilt and jewelled. Height 7½ inches. Provenance: Nepal. *Now in the collection of Mr. Christmas Humphreys, London.* 9th—10th century A.D. *Photo: author.*

From the soft texture of the surface it appears that the figure was entirely finished and chased in wax and the metal cast not tooled. The figure is seated in *Padmasana* with two hands in the front holding the Buddhist gesture of *The Wheel of the Law.* The back right hand is in the gesture of holding a lotus or rosary and the left holding the sacred book.

9. VISHNU. Copper gilt. Height 44.6cm. Provenance: Nepal. *Now at the Museum of Fine Arts, Boston.* 9th—10th century A.D. *Photo: courtesy, Museum of Fine Arts, Boston.*

The figure represents the divinity of preservation. It holds a fruit in the lower right hand and a conch in the lower left. The upper right hand (now broken) probably held a discus and the upper left a mace (broken away).

10. WHITE TARA. Copper gilt. Height 8 inches. Provenance: Tibet. *Now in the collection of Mr. Christmas Humphreys, London.* 15th—16th century A.D. *Photo: author.*

This is an excellent example of casting in *cire perdue* and it shows careful chasing all round the figure which makes it appear as the work of a goldsmith. But in spite of over-engraving the figure exhibits sculptural beauty. The White Tara goddess is believed to have been incarnated in the Chinese wife of the Tibetan king Srong-rsangampo. According to tradition she was of white complexion. The symbol of White Tara is fully blown lotuses which rise beside her shoulders.

11. GREEN TARA. Copper gilt. Height 15½ inches. Provenance: Nepal or Tibet. *Now in Indian Museum, Calcutta.* 15th—16th century A.D. *Photo: by kind permission of the Trustees of the Indian Museum, Calcutta.*

   The figure is admirably modelled and seated in an easy and graceful attitude. The Green Tara goddess is believed to have been incarnated in the Nepalese wife of the Tibetan king Srong-rsangampo. She is usually shown seated in *Ardhaparyanka* attitude (i.e., with one leg partly down from the *Padmasana* or lotus seat).

12. WHITE TARA. Beaten copper gilt and jewelled. Height 30 inches. Provenance: Nepal. *Now in the Indian Section, Victoria and Albert Museum, London.* 16th—17th century A.D. *Photo: author.*

   This is a fine example of large-size repoussé work in the round. The head and arms were made separately, then joined together. Although it has been shaped out entirely by hammering, the figure displays refined form and plastic beauty.

13. DIPA-LAKSHMI. Bronze. Height 12 inches. Provenance: Bengal. *Now at British Museum, London.* 16th century A.D. *Photo: courtesy, British Museum.*

   This somewhat crudely shaped but monumental type statuette reminds one of clay figures still made by the folk artists of Bengal. The closed hands are fashioned to clasp a burner which is missing.

14. PRINCESS WITH SEVEN ATTENDANTS. Bronze. Dimension: 9.5cm. (including the ring) x 9.6cm. Provenance: North India. *Now at Museum of Fine Arts, Boston.* Mid-seventeenth century A.D. *Photo: courtesy, Museum of Fine Arts, Boston.*

   The plaque shows very low relief with a dominant effect of painting rather than sculpture.

15. HORSE AND RIDER. Brass. Height 44cm. Provenance: Bharatpur, Rajputana. *Now in the collection of Lt. Col. John Watson, Burley, Hants.* 19th century A.D. *Photo: courtesy, Royal Academy of Arts, London.*

This equestrian statuette has the quality of a monumental figure. Compared with the virile and animated horse the rider appears lifeless and stiff.

16. WARRIOR RIDING A BLACK BUCK. Brass. Height 15cm. Provenance: Bihar. *Now in the collection of Mr. John Irwin, London.* 19th century A.D. *Photo: courtesy, Royal Academy of Arts, London.*

This comical rider and animal show the humour and vitality of folk-art at its best. It contains very skilful workmanship in metal craft.

17. THE TIRTHANKARA PARSANATHA. Bronze or copper. Height 7 inches. Provenance: unknown, probably the Deccan. *Now at British Museum, London.* 12th century A.D. *Photo: courtesy, British Museum.*

The figure of the saint is seated in meditation. Individually the figures appear crudely shaped but together they produce a massive architectonic effect. A god and a goddess are seen seated beneath the saint (probably Indra and his consort) and below them are eight child-like standing figures probably representing the *Astavasu* (guardians of the eight regions).

18. NEMINATHA. Bronze. Height 58cm. Provenance: East Khandesh, Bombay. *Now at Prince of Wales Museum, Bombay.* 9th century A.D. *Photo: courtesy, Royal Academy of Arts, London.*

Neminatha is seen surrounded by 23 other Tirthankaras or Jain saints, attendants, divinities and heavenly musicians. The whole composition shows the architectural effect of the façade of a temple.

19. FEMALE LAMP-HOLDER. Bronze gilt. Height 15.5cm. Provenance: Hyderabad State. *Now at Government Museum, Hyderabad.* 8th—9th century A.D. *Photo: courtesy, Royal Academy of Arts, London.*

Simple and compact design with considerable monumental quality.

20. JAIN GODDESS. Bronze. Height 33cm. Provenance: Mysore. *Now in the collection of Capt. Jones, London.* 10th century A.D. *Photo: courtesy, Royal Academy of Arts, London.*

21. DIPA-LAKSHMI. Brass. Height 10½ inches. Provenance: Hyderabad. *Now in the Indian Section, Victoria and Albert Museum, London.* 19th century A.D. *Photo: author.*

22. DIPA-LAKSHMI. Brass. Height 15 inches. Provenance: Hyderabad. *Now in the Indian Section, Victoria and Albert Museum, London.* 19th century A.D. *Photo: author.*

23. EQUESTRIAN FIGURE. Brass. Height 6¾ inches. Provenance: Vizagapatam. *Now in the Indian Section, Victoria and Albert Museum, London.* 19th century. *Photo: author.*

24. EQUESTRIAN FIGURES. Brass. Height 4 inches. Provenance: Vizagapatam. *Now in the Indian Section, Victoria and Albert Museum, London.* 19th century A.D. *Photo: author.*

These excellent metal statuettes cast in *cire perdue* are seen wearing the contemporary costume of the Deccanese cavalry. The modelling of these figures is naturalistic and full of movement.

25. ELEPHANT WITH RIDERS. Brass. Height 8 inches. Provenance: Vizagapatam. *Now in the Indian Section, Victoria and Albert Museum, London.* 19th century A.D. *Photo: author.*

26. ELEPHANT WITH RIDERS. Brass. Height 6¼ inches. Provenance: Vizagapatam. *Now in the Indian Section, Victoria and Albert Museum, London.* 19th century A.D. *Photo: author.*

27. RAMA. Bronze. Height 112cm. Provenance: Tanjore District, Madras. *Now at Government Museum, Madras.* 10th—11th century A.D. *Photo: courtesy, Royal Academy of Arts, London.*

The figure represents the hero of the epic Ramayana. Its loin-cloth is closely tied to the body and supported by a girdle with a mask-like *Kirtimukha*. The raised left hand shows the gesture of holding a bow, and the right an arrow. The figure wears a royal crown and ear-rings.

28. CHILD PREACHER. Copper. Height 17½ inches. Provenance: Madras. *Now in the Indian Section, Victoria and Albert Museum, London.* 10th—11th century A.D. *Photo: author.*

This figure probably represents Tiru-gnana-samabandha Swami, a Saivaite saint who when a child was said to have been called to the service of the god Siva.

29, 30. HANUMAN. Bronze. Height 60cm. Provenance: Tanjore District, Madras. *Now at Government Museum, Madras.* 11th century A.D. *Photo: courtesy, Royal Academy of Arts, London.*

The figure represents the monkey prince who served Rama in his war against Ravana, the king of Lanka (Ceylon). Except for the head and tail the figure has a human appearance. Its attitude expresses the attentive posture of a devotee awaiting his master's order.

31, 32. NATARAJA. Bronze. Height 115cm. Provenance: Tiruvelangadu, Madras. *Now at Government Museum, Madras.* 11th century A.D. *Photo: courtesy, Royal Academy of Arts, London.*

This magnificent figure of the dancing Siva shows the height of achievement in Indian metal sculpture. This three-eyed god wears on his head braided locks, a skull, a cobra, the crescent moon, a lotus and a treble Dhatura-flower. In his right ear is a man's earring, in the left a woman's. He has four arms bifurcating at the shoulder. The upper right hand holds a drum, the upper left fire, the lower right hand is in *Abhaya mudra* (gesture of giving assurance) and the left hand is outstretched in dancing gesture. The left foot is lifted in dancing posture and the right foot is pressed upon a dwarf-like demon. There was an elliptical aureole of flame round the figure rising from the lotus pedestal which is now missing. The figure appears to have been well chased in its wax model and then tooled on the metal cast.

33. THE BUDDHA. Bronze. Height 74.5cm. Provenance: Negapatam, Madras. *Now at Government Museum, Madras.* 11th—12th century A.D. *Photo: courtesy, Royal Academy of Arts, London.*

The figure is seated in meditation (*Padmasana*) and attended by two Nagas (regents of water) holding fly-whisks. The robe is extremely diaphanous and closely clinging to the body, thus revealing the form. The nimbus behind its head is rimmed with flames. The small umbrella and the decorative tree-motif with lotuses above its head signify the divine nativity and the princely origin of the Buddha. The composition is well balanced and the decorative elements are elegantly restrained.

34. THE BUDDHA. Copper. Height 7 inches. Provenance: Negapatam, Madras. *Now at British Museum, London.* 11th—12th century A.D. *Photo: courtesy, British Museum.*

35. KANNAPPA NAYANAR. Bronze. Height 48.5cm. Provenance: Chittoor District, Madras. *Now at Government Museum, Madras.* 12th century A.D. *Photo: courtesy, Royal Academy of Arts, London.*

The figure represents a Saiva saint. Its hands are folded in prayer and the loin-cloth is supported by a girdle from which a dagger hangs on the right side.

36. JAIN TIRTHANKARA. Bronze. Height 8 inches. Provenance: South India. *Now at British Museum, London.* 12th century A.D. *Photo: courtesy, British Museum.*

This figure stands in yogic attitude and shows monolithic monumental quality.

37. AIYANAR. Bronze. Height 8 inches. Provenance: South India. *Now at British Museum, London.* 12th century A.D. *Photo: courtesy, British Museum.*

The figure represents the god commander of the heavenly hosts. According to mythology he was born of the union of Siva and Mohini (a female aspect of Vishnu). The left hand is in the gesture of holding a bow and the right an arrow. It wears braided hair forming a massive crown.

38. UMA. Bronze. Height 42.2cm. Provenance: South India. *Now at Museum of Fine Arts, Boston.* 12th—13th century A.D. *Photo: courtesy, Royal Academy of Arts, London.*

The statuette is seen seated in *Ardhaparyanka asana* with its left leg pendent. The right hand is in *Kataka* gesture (gesture of discourse) and the left in *Varada*, i.e., the gesture of charity. It wears a high crown and its body above the waist is nude except for jewelry. The bronze is well proportioned.

39. DANCING KRISHNA. Bronze. Height $14\frac{1}{2}$ inches. Provenance: South India. *Now in the Indian Section, Victoria and Albert Museum, London.* 12th—13th century A.D. *Photo: author.*

The child god is nude except for jewelry and the girdle round the waist. The arms and legs are gracefully poised and express rhythmic movement.

40. CHOLA KING. Bronze. Height 74cm. Provenance: Chingleput, Madras. *Now in the collection of Mr. Gautam Sarabhai, Ahmedabad, India.* 13th century A.D. *Photo: courtesy, Royal Academy of Arts, London.*

This effigy of a Chola king with its hands folded in prayer holds a lotus between the palms. It is nude except for the brief clinging lion-cloth and jewelry. Although the muscular details of the figure are seen suppressed it expresses immense strength and vitality.

41. CHOLA QUEEN. Bronze. Height 53.5cm. Provenance: Chingleput District, Madras. *Now in the collection of Mr. Gautam Sarabhai, Ahmedabad.* 13th century A.D. *Photo: courtesy, Royal Academy of Arts, London.*

This richly garbed and jewelled effigy of a Chola queen stands gracefully on a lotus pedestal. The fluid contour line of the superb sculpture transforms hard metal into soft, living flesh. The fine engraving of the drapery produces an effect of richly decorated silk.

The left hand is in the gesture of holding a lotus and the right hangs down to the side in relaxed position.

42. PARVATI AS MATANGI. Bronze. Height 65.5cm. Provenance: Tanjore District, Madras. *Now in the collection of Mr. Gautam Sarabhai, Ahmedabad.* 13th century A.D. *Photo: courtesy, Royal Academy of Arts, London.*

The hand gesture signifies that the figure is playing with a ball, throwing and catching it between the hands. The slightly stooping position of the body expresses well the balancing attitude of the figure engaged in the game. The limbs are well shaped and their relative proportions are admirably fashioned.

43. PARVATI. Bronze. Height 61.5cm. Provenance: South India. *Now in the collection of Sir Cowasji Jehangir, G.B.E., K.C.I.E., Bombay.* 13th—14th century A.D. *Photo: courtesy, Royal Academy of Arts, London.*

44. NANDISA. Bronze. Height 72cm. Provenance: South India. *Now in the collection of Sir Cowasji Jehangir, G.B.E., K.C.I.E., Bombay.* 13th—14th century A.D. *Photo: courtesy, Royal Academy of Arts, London.*

The figure represents a demi-god attendant of Siva with four arms. The front right and left hands are folded as if in prayer, the rear right hand holds an axe (now broken) and the rear left hand holds a jumping antelope. The upbraided hair is piled high and bears a crescent moon.

45. SIVA KANKALAMURTI. Bronze. Height 34cm. Provenance: Tanjore District, Madras. *Now at Government Museum, Madras.* 13th—14th century A.D. *Photo: courtesy, Royal Academy of Arts, London.*

This is an aspect of Siva with four arms. The front left hand holds a drum and the front right hand is in the act of beating the drum with a stick. An antelope is seen leaping towards the rear right hand which holds a communicative gesture. There is a crescent moon on the high braided hair of the figure.

46. TAMIL SAIVA SAINT. Bronze. Height 22½ inches. Provenance: South India. *Now at British Museum, London.* 14th century A.D. *Photo: courtesy, British Museum.*

The figure represents the Saiva saint Manikkavachaka. It wears no jewelry. The hair is piled round the back of the head in a huge bun. The left hand holds the sacred book and the right is in the gesture of discourse.

43

47. PARVATI. Bronze. Height $26\frac{1}{2}$ inches. Provenance: Madras Presidency. *Now in the Indian Section, Victoria and Albert Museum, London.* 14th—15th century A.D. *Photo: courtesy, Victoria and Albert Museum.*

48. AIYANAR. Bronze. Height 10 inches. Provenance: South India. *Now in the Indian Section, Victoria and Albert Museum, London.* 14th—15th century A.D. *Photo: courtesy, Indian Section, Victoria and Albert Museum.*

   The figure is seated in *Maharajalila* attitude. The right hand holds an elephant goad. The braided hair falls at the back of the head in tiers on each side.

49. SOMASKANDA. Bronze. Height 43cm. Provenance: Tanjore District, Madras. *Now at National Museum, Copenhagen.* 14th—15th century A.D. *Photo: courtesy, National Museum, Copenhagen.*

   This figure of Siva is one of a group sculpture on the same pedestal showing Uma on Siva's left and their son Skanda (which is now missing) between them. The symbols and gestures of the figure are similar to those of Fig. 39 except that the front right hand is in the gesture of assurance and the left in the gesture of discourse.

50. UMA. Bronze. Height 36cm. Provenance: Tanjore District, Madras. *Now at National Museum, Copenhagen.* 14th—15th century A.D. *Photo: courtesy, National Museum, Copenhagen.*

   The figure is one of the group on the same pedestal with the figure of Siva illustrated in Fig. 49. She represents Uma or Parvati, the consort of Siva. The figure is gracefully poised on the lotus pedestal in *Lalitasana* attitude, with its left hand denoting the gesture of discourse or holding a lotus.

51. BOY SAIVA SAINT. Copper. Height 0.465m. Provenance: South India. *Now at Museum of Fine Arts, Boston.* 14th century A.D. *Photo: courtesy, Museum of Fine Arts, Boston.*

   This figure probably represents the Saiva saint, Tiru Jnana Sambandha Swami. It is nude except for scanty jewelry. The modelling and tactile quality of the figure are excellent.

52. A VAISHNAVA DEVOTEE. Bronze. Height $16\frac{1}{2}$ inches. Provenance: South India. *Now in the Indian Section, Victoria and Albert Museum, London.* 14th—15th century A.D. *Photo: courtesy, Victoria and Albert Museum.*

53. DEVI AS UMA. Copper. Height 59cm. Provenance: South India. *Now at Museum of Fine Arts, Boston.* 14th—15th century A.D. *Photo: courtesy, Museum of Fine Arts, Boston.*

The figure stands gracefully in *Abhanga* pose. The body above the waist is nude except for jewelry. The apparel below the waist is finely engraved and appears as printed silk or brocade. The right hand is raised and in *Kataka* pose (gesture of discourse) and the left is pendent.

54. KING KRINSHNARAYA AND HIS QUEENS. Brass. Height life-size. Provenance: Chitoor District, South India. *Now at Srinivasa Perumal Temple at Tirumalai, Tirrupati Chitoor District.* 16th century A.D. *Photo: courtesy, Archaeological Survey of India.*

The figure of the king is standing in *Samapada* pose. The body is bare except for the jewelry and the short *Dhoti* which covers the waist and the thighs. The hands are folded in prayer. The king wears a high cap-like crown. The figures of the queens are gracefully poised in an attitude complimentary to each other. Both the queens are shown wearing fine silk Sarees which cover the lower half of their bodies as well as the breasts and shoulders but revealing the form. The hands of the two figures are also folded in prayer. These statues are the unique examples of large-size repoussé work in the round. These figures do not reveal any effect of plastic modelling but in their well-fashioned form the metallic quality and sculptural stability are expressive. On the right shoulder of each figure can be seen an inscription showing its identity.

55. NATARAJA. Copper. Height 91.5cm. Provenance: South India. *Now at Museum of Fine Arts, Boston.* 16th century A.D. *Photo: courtesy, Museum of Fine Arts, Boston.*

In this fine example of Nataraja the limbs are well balanced and rhythmically poised. The locks of its matted hair are flung on the sides of its head depicting whirling motion. The figure wears a ribbed or striped loin-cloth supported by a sash round the waist which is knotted at both sides with its ends reaching to the head and foot of the dwarf under Nataraja's foot. Dr. Coomaraswamy quotes about the symbolism of Nataraja as follows: " Creation arises from the drum (as sound is the primal manifestation of creative energy); protection proceeds from the assuring hand (i.e., the lower right hand in *Abhaya* position, signifying ' Fear not '); from the fire proceeds destruction; from the planted foot illusion; the upraised foot bestows salvation. The front left hand points to the lifted foot to indicate the refuge of the individual soul."

56, 57. BALAKRISHNA. Copper. Height 12 inches. Provenance: South India. *Now in the Indian Section, Victoria and Albert Museum, London.* 16th—17th century A.D. *Photo: author.*

The figure is nude except for the waistband with bells and jewelry. The object in its right hand represents a ball of butter which the child Krishna it is said was very fond of eating. The left arm is poised in dance gesture.

58. LAKSHMI. Brass. Height 25½ inches. Provenance: Mysore. *Now in the Indian Section, Victoria and Albert Museum, London.* 16th—17th century A.D. *Photo: author.*

Rather crude in proportion the figure shows monumental and massive quality.

59. GANESA. Bronze. Height 66.5cm. Provenance: South India. *Now in the collection of Sir Cowasji Jehangir, G.B.E., K.C.I.E., Bombay.* 18th century A.D. *Photo: courtesy, Royal Academy of Arts, London.*

The figure represents the elephant-headed son of Siva and Parvati. He is always represented as a pot-bellied dwarf, usually with four arms, his vehicle being the rat. He is regarded as the Remover of all difficulties and is invoked at the commencement of almost all Brahmanical religious ceremonies. His attributes are the elephant goad and rosary. The front right hand of the figure illustrated holds a broken tusk, the left holds a ball of sweet. The back right hand holds an elephant goad (now missing) and the back left hand holds a noose.

60. EQUESTRIAN FIGURE. Bronze. Height 20.5cm. Provenance: Mysore. *Now in the collection of Archaeological Department, Mysore State.* 19th century A.D. *Photo: courtesy, Royal Academy of Arts, London.*

This humorous figure of a woman on a donkey expresses the unsophisticated delight of folk-art. It wears a lotus-like crown and holds in the left hand an object which appears to be a bell.

61. SIVA ON HIS VEHICLE NANDI THE BULL. Bronze. Height 8½ inches. Provenance: South India. *Now in the Indian Section, Victoria and Albert Museum, London.* 19th century A.D. *Photo: author.*

The attitude and attributes shown here are similar to that of the figure in Fig. 44. The figure of Siva lacks refinement and life but the bull shows excellent form, vitality and movement.

1. Young couple.
Gold-repoussé, lac filled.
TAXILA.

2. Bull. *Bronze.*
GHANDARA.

3. Brahma. *Bronze gilt and inlaid with copper.* SIND.

4. Avalokitesvara. *Copper gilt and jewelled with jacinth.* NEPAL.

5. Balarama, Lakshmi, and Vasudeva. *Bronze*. BENGAL.

6. Siva and Uma. *Brass*. BENGAL.

7. Lokulisha (?). *Copper gilt.* BIHAR (?)

8. Prajnaparamita (?). *Copper gilt and jewelled.* NEPAL.

9. Vishnu. *Copper gilt*. NEPAL.

10. White Tara. *Copper gilt.* TIBET.

11. Green Tara. *Copper gilt.* NEPAL OR TIBET.

12.   White Tara. *Beaten copper gilt and jewelled.* NEPAL.

13. Dipa-Lakshmi. *Bronze.* BENGAL.

14. Princess with Seven Attendants. *Bronze.* NORTH INDIA.

15.   Horse and Rider.   *Brass*.   RAJPUTANA.

16.   Warrior riding a Black Buck.   *Brass*.   BIHAR.

17.   The Tirthankara Parsanatha.   *Bronze or copper.*   DECCAN (?)

18. Neminatha. *Bronze.* EAST KHANDESH.

19. Female Lamp-holder. *Bronze gilt.*

20. Jain Goddess. *Bronze.* MYSORE.

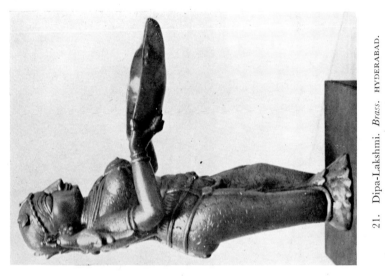

21. Dipa-Lakshmi. *Brass.* HYDERABAD.

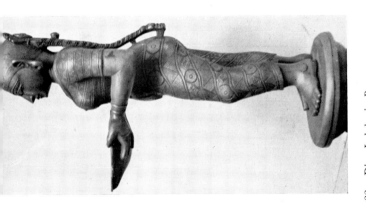

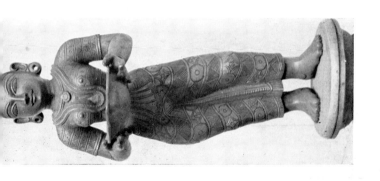

22. Dipa-Lakshmi. *Brass.* HYDERABAD.

23. Equestrian figure.
Brass. VIZAGAPATAM.

24. Equestrian figures.
Brass. VIZAGAPATAM.

25. Elephant with riders. *Brass.*
VIZAGAPATAM.

26. Elephant with riders. *Brass.*
VIZAGAPATAM.

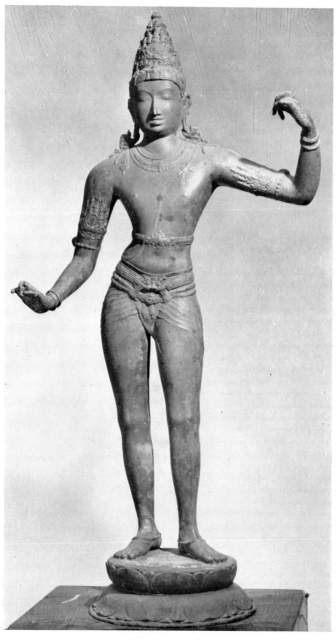

27. Rama. *Bronze*. MADRAS.

28.   Child preacher. *Copper*. MADRĄS,

29. Hanuman. *Bronze*. MADRAS.

30. *Side view of figure* 29.

31. Nataraja. *Bronze*. MADRAS.

32. *Back view of figure* 31.

33. The Buddha. *Bronze*. MADRAS.

34. The Buddha. *Copper*. MADRAS.

35. Kannappa Nayanar.
Bronze. MADRAS.

36. Jain Tirthankara.
Bronze. SOUTH INDIA.

37. Aiyanar. *Bronze.* SOUTH INDIA.

38. Uma. *Bronze*. SOUTH INDIA.

39. Dancing Krishna. *Bronze*. SOUTH INDIA.

40. Chola King. *Bronze*. MADRAS.

41.   Chola Queen. *Bronze*. MADRAS.

42. Parvati as Matangi.
Bronze. MADRAS.

43. Parvati. *Bronze*.
SOUTH INDIA.

44. Nandisa. *Bronze*. SOUTH INDIA.

45. Siva Kankalamurti. *Bronze*. MADRAS,

46. Tamil Saiva Saint. *Bronze.* SOUTH INDIA,

47. Parvati. *Bronze*. MADRAS.

48. Aiyanar. *Bronze*. SOUTH INDIA.

49. Somaskanda. *Bronze.* MADRAS,

50. Uma. *Bronze*. MADRAS.

51. Boy Saiva Saint. *Copper.* SOUTH INDIA.

52.   A Vaishnava devotee.   *Bronze*.   SOUTH INDIA.

53. Devi as Uma. *Copper*. SOUTH INDIA.

54. King Krinshnaraya and his Queens. *Brass*. SOUTH INDIA.

55. Nataraja. *Copper.* SOUTH INDIA.

56. Balakrishna. *Copper*. SOUTH INDIA.

57. *Back view of figure 56.*

58. Lakshmi. *Brass.* MYSORE.

59. Ganesa. *Bronze*. SOUTH INDIA.

60. Equestrian figure. *Bronze*. MYSORE.

61. Siva on his vehicle, Nandi the Bull. *Bronze*. SOUTH INDIA.